Glances

Haiku for now

Ellis Potter

© 2022 Ellis Potter

Without limiting the rights under copyright reserved above, no part of this publication may be reproduced, stored in, or introduced into a retrieval system, or transmitted in any form by any means (electronic, mechanical, photocopying, or otherwise), without the prior written permission from the publisher, except where permitted by law, and except in the case of brief quotations embodied in critical articles and reviews. For information, write: info@destineemedia.com

Reasonable care has been taken to trace original sources and copyright holders for any quotations appearing in this book. Should any attribution be found to be incorrect or incomplete, the publisher welcomes written documentation supporting correction for subsequent printing.

Published by: Destinee Media
www.destineemedia.com

Illustration by: Ben Stone
Layout by: Ben Stone

All rights reserved by the author.
ISBN 978-1-938367-71-7

Table of Contents

Introduction - 7	Clear Night - 32
Part One:	Comfort - 34
Activity - 8	Confusion - 36
Age - 10	Covid - 38
Alps - 12	Culture - 40
Alternative - 14	Dance - 42
Architecture - 16	Death of Wife - 44
Autumn - 18	Dull - 46
Bible - 20	Fireworks - 48
Bird Feeder - 22	Flight - 50
Birthday - 24	Friends - 52
Boating - 26	Garden - 54
Changing - 28	Guardians - 56
Choices - 30	Hedonism - 58

Hiking	60	Question	88
Honey	62	Smoked Glass	90
Hurry	64	Spirit	92
In the Night	66	Splash	94
Instinct	68	Spring	96
L'Abri	70	Summer	98
Mirror	72	Tenacity	100
Moonshine	74	The Matrix	102
Nature	76	Vision	104
Night Life	78	Water	106
Opportunists	80	Wind	108
Paintings	82	Winter	110
Poetry	84	**Part Two:**	
Puberty	86	Proverbs	112

Introduction

The Haiku is an old Japanese short poetry form consisting of 3 lines of 5, 7 and 5 syllables, which usually don't rhyme. The Haiku are mostly about nature and usually hint at the season of the year. They paint a picture and/or tell a story, with the last line being a surprise or conclusion. Because they are so short, they can be seen at a glance. They are short moments that open the mind and heart to awareness. When the writer is faithful to the strict form, the shape and rhythm of the Haiku are freely recognized and received by the reader. Most of the poems in this book are expressions of my own experiences and observations. Hopefully you can share in these experiences and remember some of your own. Perhaps these poems will make you more open and receptive to experience of nature in the future.

Ellis Potter
Basel, 2022

Activity

Squirrels in the trees
Jumping, racing, cavorting
Making a fur whirr.

Age

Sun on old woman
We see warm colors beauty
She sees dark and cold

Alps

Alpine meadows, a
Rolling vastness of pristine
Diminuity.

Alternative

Meditation for
Self-help and comfort. Jesus
For Grace and new life.

Architecture

Big city buildings
Dancing around each other
Like giants in Spring

Autumn

Dry leaves blowing a
Round in swirly whirls and piles
Making way for Spring

Bible

Reading the Bible
Struggle for understanding
Peace given through faith

Bird Feeder

Friends and enemies
Parade in feathered drama
In kitchen window

Birthday

Sprightly spring fawn child
Steps lightly into summer
A more measured pace

Boating

Floating on the lake
Trailing fingers in water
Hold hands with myself

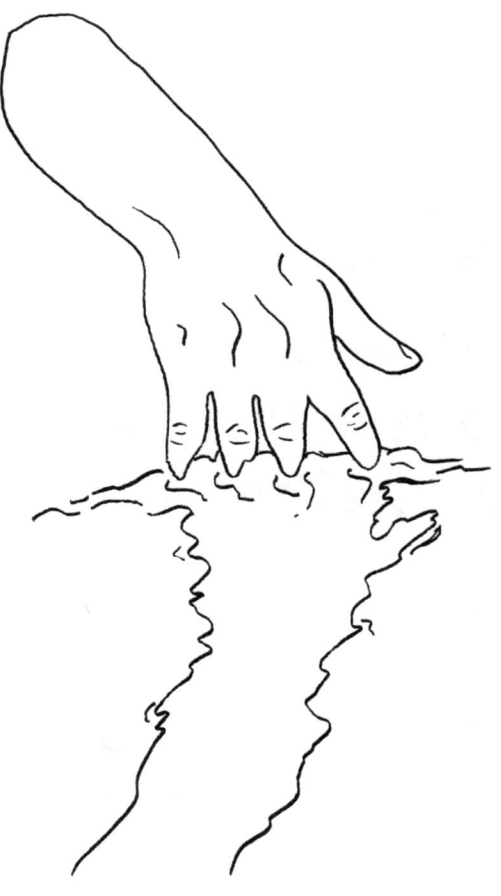

Changing

Nature as quiet
As leaves changing their colors
Preparing for sleep

Choices

For other or self
Writing on eternity
With good or evil.

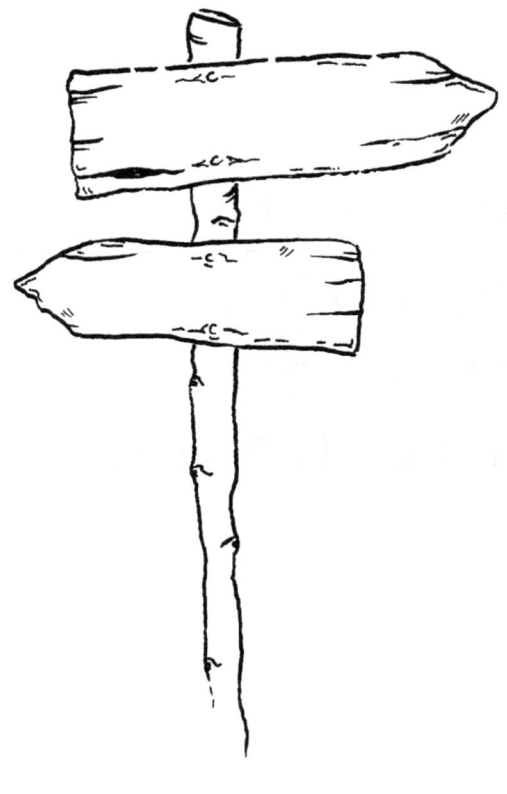

Clear Night

A blanket of stars
God will unzip the cover
And come bursting in

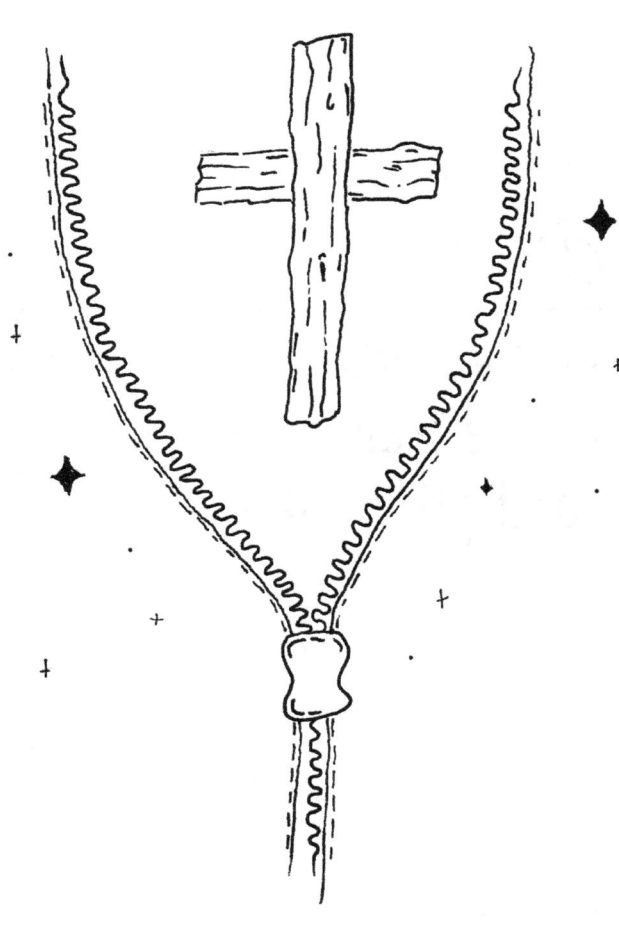

Comfort

Even a hard rock
Is a welcome resting place
For the tired hiker

Confusion

Snowfall in springtime
Is moving us both forward
And backward in time

Covid

The plague is raging
Everyone is in danger
Hearts flutter or freeze

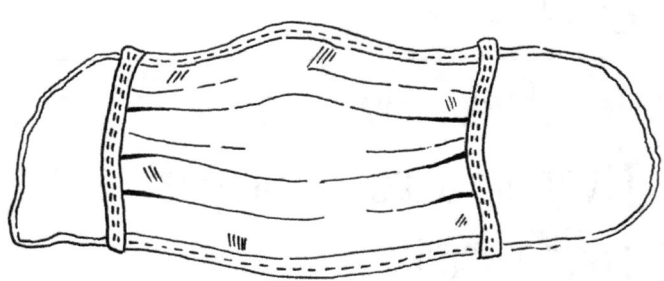

Culture

Jet black crows argue
Over garbage in the park
High society.

Dance

The dancer moves
In unnecessary gestures
Making life human.

Death of Wife

Magnolia blossom
Giving beauty and fragrance
Fades into freshness

Dull

Foggy day and dis -
Orientation make me
Wonder where I am

Fireworks

Dead looking branches
Exploding and colorful
Every year in Spring

Flight

Like a bird flying
High because it can do it
Prayer completes us

Friends

Eating and laughing
Friends give each other lightness
In a darkened world.

Garden

Seeds under the ground
Seeking light out of darkness
Do we do the same?

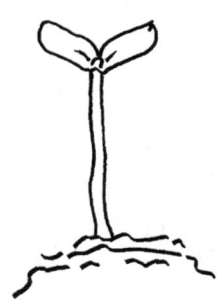

Guardians

Poplar trees in rows
Green soldiers at attention
Holding up the sky

Hedonism

Cats on warm stone wall
Prime demonstration of the
Enjoyment of life

Hiking

Vast mountain ranges
Tiny flowers and insects
Seen through the same eyes

Honey

Zooming here and there
Bees are buzzing busily
Gathering sweetness

Hurry

Rain is everywhere
Umbrella is forgotten
Run between the drops!

In the Night

Ambulance siren
Someone in emergency
Hope they are OK

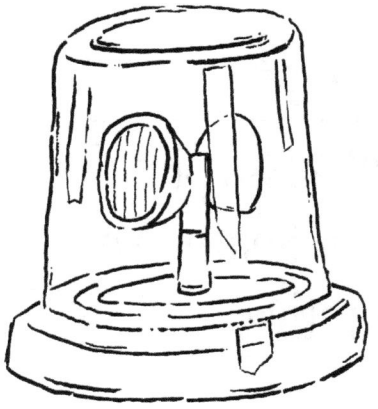

Instinct

Vees of geese pointing
North or South. Very advanced
Cooperatives.

L'Abri

People coming here
Brought by God for His blessing
Workers watch and pray

Mirror

Apple blossoms bloom
And fall always in the world
And inside my mind

Moonshine

Full moon looking down
Sees all our darkest secrets
Silence is golden

Nature

Warning and fighting
Push and shove and chase away
Morning birds singing

Night Life

Danger in the garden
Terror lurks on every side
Kitties on the prowl

Opportunists

Graceful high steppers
Grateful gleaners parading
Storks follow the plow

Paintings

Looking at paintings
Color and form are speaking
What are they saying?

Poetry

Life is very big
Poets see the whole and the part
Writing just enough

Puberty

Rocks have no pimples
Trashcans have no emotions
Aren't they lucky?

Question

Who prowls through the woods?
Who slinks and hides in darkness?
The owl wants to know.

Smoked Glass

Purely Beginning
Burning through various deaths
Our hearts turn to ice

Falsely beginning
Purified by Spirit's fire
Our hearts melt to flesh.

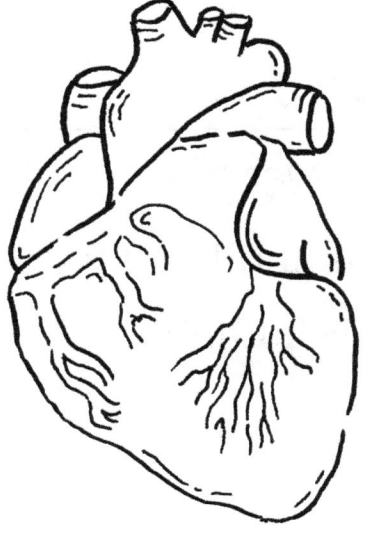

Spirit

Flute player blowing
Space and time in harmony.
Music is human.

Splash

Early May sunshine
Brings the first customer to
The window birdbath

Spring

Violent springtime
Pushing everything around
Tiny buds are strong

Summer

Shimmering heatwaves
Make everything fantasy
See and don't believe

Tenacity

Windstorm in the hills
Tiny flowers in the rocks
Clinging for dear life

The Matrix

Breezes blow outside
Birds flit around their feeder
Time does not move

Vision

See reality
Objective and subjective
In and out of mind.

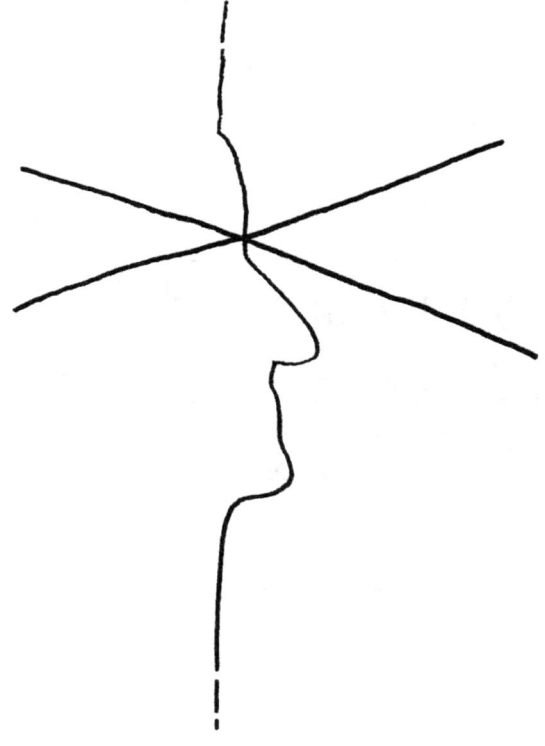

Water

Water runs in streets
Along the streams and brooks and
In the kitchen sink.

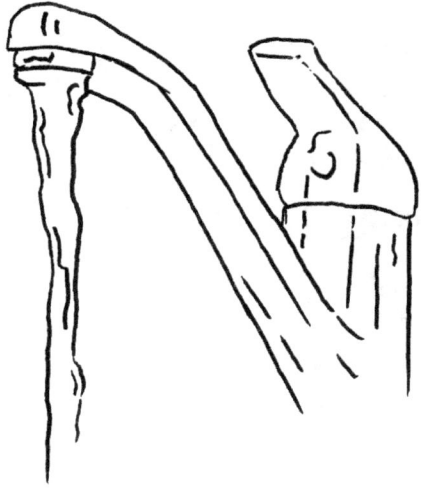

Wind

Rushing here and there
Wind is air in a hurry
Don't get blown away

Winter

Brittle icy cold
Snow blanket keeps the world still
Sleep is good for you

Proverbs

Proverbs (words put forward) are usually shorter than Haiku with no standard structure. Proverbs tend to have a point or message and are intended to teach or guide the reader. They often express cultural wisdom or morals. Proverbs are more often metaphorical, while Haiku are a more direct observation or experience. Proverbs are generally a clear rational statement, while Haiku are more experiential, and true in non-intellectual ways. Most of this short collection are originally mine, while a few are adaptations of something I've read or heard.

Ellis H. Potter
Basel, 2022.

God does nature.
People do art.

100% God's sovereignty
+ 100% human free will
= 200% Reality.

The Bible should not be taken in homeopathic doses,
But in whole nourishing meals.

Good music repays both a casual and a careful listening.

If God got rid of evil,
What would He do with you?

Meaning depends on limits.
If I overcome all my limits,
do I become meaningless?

Trust, not resources
Is the foundation of
a nation's wealth.

Only ignorant questions are honest. They open the possibility of learning for the asker.

They told me I can be anything
I want to be.
So, I became a problem.

We can't be spiritual
without a physical body.
Jesus isn't.

Without guilt there is no hope.

Time is created,
Expressing eternity, where God lives.

Getting a tattoo is like
Putting a bumper sticker
on a Ferrari.

If we listen louder than we talk
We might learn something.

Be like a little child,
Hungry to experience reality.

Meet people at their level of Development, not yours.

True identity is not in the self,
But in relationships with others.

Blessings are for growth,
Pleasant or painful.

Life is put on pause by death.
Christians say, "see you later".

Spiritual means totally real,
Not only supernatural.

Read what is false.
It puts the truth in sharper focus.

www.ingramcontent.com/pod-product-compliance
Lightning Source LLC
Chambersburg PA
CBHW051737290426
43673CB00102B/460/J